12 Easy Knitting Projects

Peg Blanchette & Terri Thibault

ILLUSTRATIONS BY NORMA JEAN MARTIN-JOURDENAIS

Quick Starts for Kids!®

Williamson Books   Nashville, Tennessee

Library of Congress Cataloging-in-Publication Data

Blanchette, Peg, 1949-
  12 easy knitting projects / Peg Blanchette & Terri Thibault ; illustrations by Norma Jean Martin-Jourdenais.
      p. cm. — (Quick starts for kids!)
  Includes index.
  ISBN 0-8249-6785-2 (softcover : alk. paper) — ISBN 0-8249-6784-4 (casebound : alk. paper)
  1. Knitting—Juvenile literature. 2. Knitting—Patterns—Juvenile literature. I. Title: Twelve easy knitting projects. II. Thibault, Terri, 1954- III. Title. IV. Series.
  TT820.B6423 2006
  746.43'2—dc22

                              2005029247

Dedication
We dedicate this book
to our sisters:
Debbie Lavalette (Terri's)
and Betsy Conlon (Peg's).
We love them dearly for their
inspiration, their faithfulness,
their encouragement,
and their ability to make us laugh,
even when we think we can't.
We depend on them as sisters
and we cherish them as friends.

Quick Starts for Kids!® series editor: **Susan Williamson**
Project editor: **Vicky Congdon**
Interior design: **Linda Williamson**, *DawsonDesign*
Front cover design and illustration: **Michael Kline**
Back cover design: **Marie Ferrante-Doyle**
Back cover and interior illustrations: **Norma Jean Martin-Jourdenais**

Published by Williamson Books
An imprint of Ideals Publications
535 Metroplex Drive, Suite 250
Nashville, Tennessee 37211
800-586-2572

CONTENTS

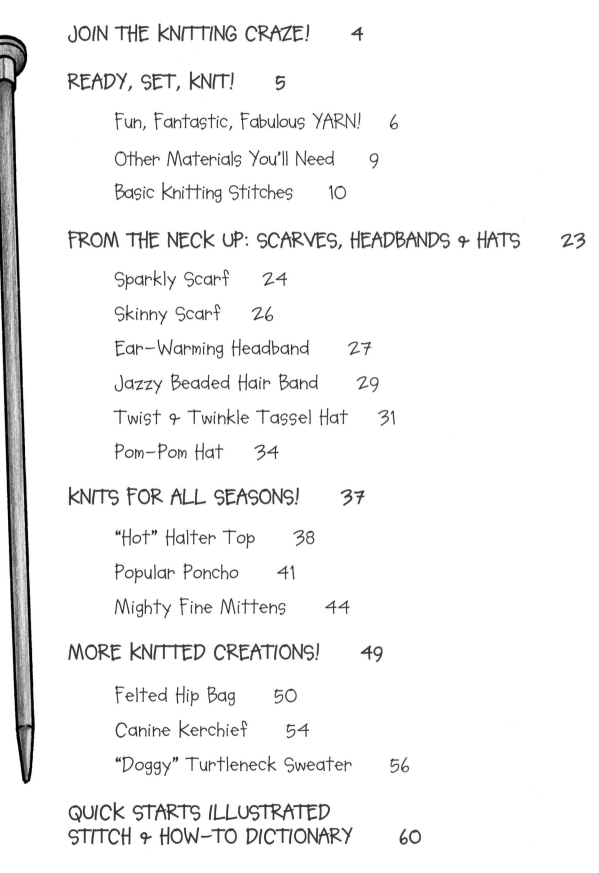

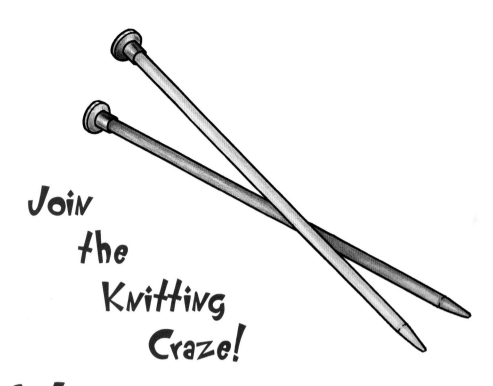

Join the Knitting Craze!

Y ou only have to flip through this book to see that we just love to knit! Peg inherited her love of knitting from her grandmother, and Terri's mother taught her to knit when she was a little girl. In 2001, Peg gathered her favorite beginning knitting projects into a **Quick Starts for Kids!**® book called *Kids Easy Knitting Projects*. Since then, there has been an incredible explosion of new colors and textures in the knitting world. To share some of these exciting new materials with you (and because crafts are always more fun with a friend!), we collaborated to bring you a collection of the latest knitting styles that are fun whether you're a beginner or you already love to knit.

Craft and hobby shops today are carrying yarn that appeals to everyone's tastes. Whether you want to be bold and sporty, classy and elegant, or playful and fun, there are all kinds of yarns to suit your mood and your project. We had fun combining different yarns (the old with the new) and seeing how they complemented each other. After you have some experience with these new yarns, you'll want to experiment with them, too. You might want to use a lighter-weight yarn or one that's bolder in color. Whatever you decide, let your imagination be your inspiration!

Peg   Terri

Ready, Set, Knit!

If you're already a knitter, you can jump right into the projects in this book (but before you do, be sure to check out the section on pages 6 and 7 on all the latest yarns!). If you need a refresher or you've never knitted before, everything you need to know is right here.

Fun, Fantastic, Fabulous ☆ YARN! ★

Half the fun of knitting is choosing the yarn for your project! And all the new yarns available in hobby and craft stores are what got us really excited about writing this book. They have taken knitting to a whole new level — and we're riding the wave!

For those of us who are long-time knitters, we're used to the four basic weights of yarn:

BABY YARN (extremely lightweight)
SPORT YARN (lightweight)
WORSTED YARN (medium weight)
BULKY YARN (heavyweight)

Yarns still come in these weights, but now there are lots of new "novelty" types as well! Feathery yarns, yarns that sparkle and shine, confetti, eyelash, boa, and ribbon yarns — these yarns have made knitting even more fun.

When we pick out yarn for a particular project, we have two main criteria: color and texture. If we're knitting an item to wear, we also consider whether we want it thick and warm or lightweight. Simply feel a strand of yarn in the store to see if it's the weight you want and check the ply (see page 8).

Some of the new yarns are not only gorgeous, but also quite pricey. There are so many choices available, however, you can probably find something comparable that's less expensive.

If you do find an expensive yarn that you simply must have, then use it for a smaller project (like the EAR-WARMING HEADBAND on page 27) or use it as an embellishment (like the strap for the FELTED HIP BAG on page 50).

To get you inspired, here are just a few of the exciting and fun-to-knit-with yarns that we used in this book.

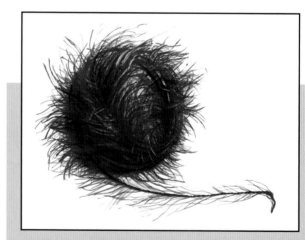

EYELASH YARN: Fine 1½" (3.5 cm) strands of shiny floss hang off this yarn, giving it an "eyelash" look and a fuzzy feel. Available with floss in both various lengths and contrasting colors. (See SPARKLY SCARF, page 24; EAR-WARMING HEADBAND, page 27; POM-POM HAT, page 34; POPULAR PONCHO, page 41; FELTED HIP BAG, page 50.)

INCHWORM:
Lightweight sport yarn with ½" (1 cm) multicolored pieces attached to the main yarn strand, giving it the appearance of a brightly colored inchworm! (See SKINNY SCARF, page 26.)

POPCORN:
The main strand of yarn is dotted with tufts of yarn in contrasting colors. (See EAR-WARMING HEADBAND, page 27.)

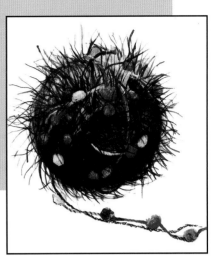

METALLIC BLEND:
Rabbit-fur softness with fine particles of metal reflecting in a complementary color. (See FELTED HIP BAG, page 50.)

SNOWDROP:
Lightweight yarn with a glistening clear plastic strand woven in that adds sparkle to your knitted creation. (See SPARKLY SCARF, page 24.)

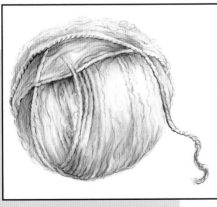

MOHAIR LOOK:
Soft, fuzzy hairlike nap covers this extremely soft yarn — it's wonderful to touch! 100% acrylic, machine washable, and durable. (See POM-POM HAT, page 34; POPULAR PONCHO, page 41; "DOGGY" TURTLENECK SWEATER, page 46.)

SUPER BULKY WEIGHT:
Very thick and easy to handle. (See TWIST & TWINKLE TASSEL HAT, page 31; MIGHTY FINE MITTENS, page 44.)

SKEINS AND BALLS

Yarn used to come in skeins (SKAYNS) that needed to be rolled into a ball to make it easier to handle. These days, a lot of yarns are already rolled into balls. Inside the ball, you'll see a loose end that you begin with (just pull on it).

If you do choose a yarn that's in a skein, you'll want to wind it into a ball so it doesn't get all tangled up while you're working. Gradually pull the yarn from the skein and wind it around a small piece of crumpled-up paper. Continue winding until you have a large ball.

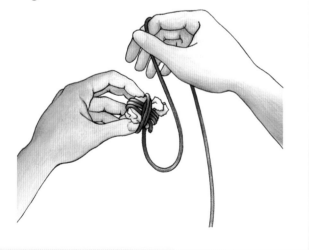

THAT HELPFUL LABEL!

Everything you need to know about your yarn is right on the label.

PLY: The ply is the number of strands twisted together, as in 2-ply, 3-ply, or 4-ply. The thicker the ply, the heavier and thicker the yarn.

WEIGHT: Knitting patterns often specify yarn by the weight of the ball or skein ("1¾ oz/50 g ball of cotton yarn") so you know how much to buy.

DYE LOT NUMBER: If you're going to buy more than one ball of yarn of a certain color, check each label for the dye lot number. Otherwise, there may be some slight color variations that will be noticeable in your finished piece.

TYPE OF YARN: To know what your yarn is made of, look for words like wool, polyester, acrylic, and cotton.

CROCHET HOOK

This simple tool is handy for picking up dropped stitches, picking up stitches along a bound-off edge (to add a fringe, for example), and adding tassels or pom-poms.

KNITTING NEEDLES

Knitting needles are available in many different lengths and sizes. The thinner the needles, the lower the number. Thin needles knit small, fine stitches, so they'll create a delicate piece. Big, thick needles make a sturdier piece with big, bold stitches.

STITCH HOLDER

Use a stitch holder to temporarily hold some stitches aside until the pattern calls for you to start knitting with them again.

YARN NEEDLE

Also called an embroidery needle, this needle has a large eye. Use it to weave in yarn ends, thread on beads and other decorative touches, and sew seams to join knitted sections.

Basic Knitting Stitches

All of the projects in this book require these four knitting skills: casting on, the knit stitch, the purl stitch, and binding off. If you already know these four knitting basics, you're ready to dive right in. If not, read on!

In the step-by-step drawings, contrasting colors are used so that you can easily see what to do with your yarn, your stitch, or your needle.

All terms are defined and illustrated in our QUICK STARTS ILLUSTRATED STITCH & HOW-TO DICTIONARY on pages 60 to 62, unless otherwise indicated.

CASTING ON

HERE'S HOW TO CREATE THE FIRST ROW OF STITCHES ON THE KNITTING NEEDLE:

Step 1:
Pull out a strand of yarn — figure about 1" (2.5 cm) per stitch. For example, if the pattern calls for casting on 40 stitches, pull out 40" (100 cm), plus an extra 5" (12.5 cm) for a yarn end.

Step 2:
Make a loose loop in the yarn as shown.

Pick up a knitting needle with your right hand* and push the needle through the loop as shown. Pull the yarn firmly, but not tightly.

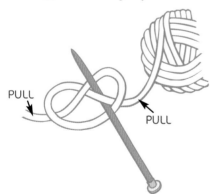

PULL

PULL

There's your first stitch!

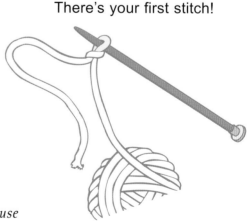

*It doesn't matter whether you are right- or left-handed. You use both hands in knitting, so follow the directions as written.

Step 3:

Holding the yarn you measured out in your left hand, wrap a strand around your left thumb as shown.

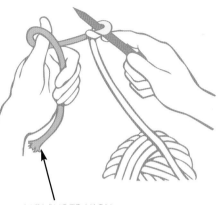

MEASURED YARN

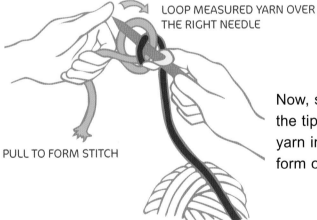

THUMB ACTS AS LEFT NEEDLE

With your thumb acting as the left needle, insert the right needle as shown.

Step 4:

Holding the yarn from the ball, called the *working yarn*, in your right hand, bring it around the tip of the right needle from back to front as shown.

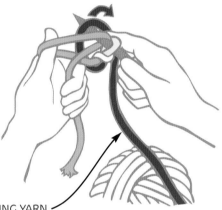

WORKING YARN

LOOP MEASURED YARN OVER THE RIGHT NEEDLE

PULL TO FORM STITCH

Now, slip the yarn from your left thumb over the tip of the right needle. Pull the measured yarn in your left hand and you'll see a stitch form on the knitting needle.

Just repeat steps 3 and 4 until you have as many stitches on the right-hand needle as you want (or as your knitting pattern calls for). Bravo! You've just cast on your first row of knitted stitches! You can slip them off the needle and simply pull them out to keep practicing for a while. Or, you can move on to learn the knit stitch.

THE KNIT STITCH

THIS STITCH WILL PROBABLY SEEM FAMILIAR BECAUSE YOU WERE REALLY ALREADY DOING IT WHEN YOU WERE CASTING ON (PAGES 10 TO 11), ONLY THIS TIME YOU'LL USE THE OTHER NEEDLE INSTEAD OF YOUR LEFT THUMB.

Step 1:

Hold the needle with the cast-on stitches in your left hand. Insert the tip of the right needle through the first stitch, under the left needle.

RIGHT NEEDLE GOES UNDER LEFT NEEDLE

Step 2:

Hold the working yarn (green) between your right index finger and thumb. (Be careful not to grab the measured yarn that you used to cast on.) From the back, bring the working yarn around the right needle and between the right and left needles.

WORKING YARN GOES OVER RIGHT NEEDLE, THEN BETWEEN BOTH

Step 3:

Slide the right needle down and pull it toward you slightly, so you can hook the yarn you just brought between the needles (the working yarn) with the tip of the right needle as shown.

NEW STITCH IS NOW ON THE RIGHT NEEDLE

Step 4:

Slide the original stitch off the left needle. See how the working yarn has formed a new stitch on the right needle?

Step 5:

Continue down the row, carefully following steps 1 through 4. When all the stitches are on the right needle, one row has been worked. How does it look — a little uneven, or nice and smooth? Try not to pull and tug at the stitches, which will make the edge of your piece look ragged. Always work the first row (the row after your cast-on row) slowly, pulling each new stitch off the left needle carefully.

Now that you've worked one row, you're ready to switch your needles so that the one with the stitches is on your left and the right one is free to start another row. Keep knitting stitches and rows until you feel comfortable with the movement of the needles and the yarn. Like anything else you practice, the more you do it, the easier it'll become.

What can you knit if you only know one stitch? Lots of things! Three different styles of scarves, for starters, plus a headband, and even an awesome hip bag! Check Contents (page 3) to get started.

Loosen up!

Sometimes when you're working a row, you may find it difficult to slip the tip of your needle inside the stitches or to slide the stitches along the needle because you've stitched them so tightly. If you give the working yarn a little tug with the right needle as you're sliding the stitch from the left needle to the right, you'll create a looser stitch that's easier to work.

THE PURL STITCH

Once you've mastered the knit stitch (pages 12 to 13), the purl stitch will seem quite easy. The secret to this stitch is to make certain that you insert your right needle correctly. After that, you'll probably recognize the steps. Here is the basic difference:

KNIT

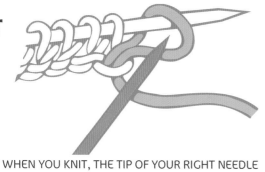

WHEN YOU KNIT, THE TIP OF YOUR RIGHT NEEDLE ENTERS EACH STITCH FACING IN THE SAME DIRECTION AS THE TIP OF THE LEFT NEEDLE.

PURL

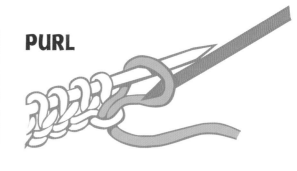

WHEN YOU PURL, BE CAREFUL TO INSERT THE TIP OF YOUR RIGHT NEEDLE INTO EACH STITCH FROM THE OPPOSITE DIRECTION.

Step 1:
Hold the working yarn in front of the piece and insert the right needle through the first stitch so the right needle is in front of the left one. (If you rest the left needle against your left index finger, you can use your left thumb to hold the right needle in place.)

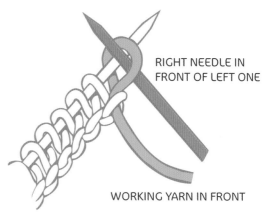

RIGHT NEEDLE IN FRONT OF LEFT ONE

WORKING YARN IN FRONT

Step 2:
Using your right hand, bring the working yarn around the right needle as shown.

Step 3:

Slide the right needle down and back, pulling the working yarn through the original stitch to form a new stitch on the right needle.

Slide the old stitch from the left needle onto the right needle.

Repeat the three purling steps until all the stitches have been worked across the row.

Here's where you may notice another difference between knitting and purling. When knitting, you start with the right needle behind the left needle and end up with the right needle in front of the left one. But when purling, the right needle starts in front of the left needle and ends up behind the left needle.

Positioning the Yarn

Oftentimes, knitting directions call for you to switch between knitting and purling, sometimes right in the same row. When you switch between stitches, remember that when you're knitting, the working yarn is always in the back of the piece. When you're purling, the working yarn is always in front of the piece.

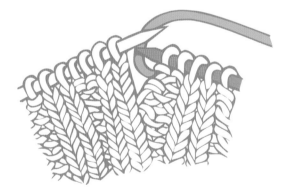

WHEN YOU SWITCH FROM PURLING TO KNITTING, MOVE THE YARN TO THE *BACK*.

WHEN YOU SWITCH FROM KNITTING TO PURLING, BRING THE YARN IN *FRONT*.

BINDING OFF

KNIT BIND OFF *(use this when the last row of stitches on the needle are knit stitches)*

Step 1:
Knit two stitches onto the right needle as if you were starting a new row of stitches.

Step 2:
Insert the left needle into the front of the first knitted stitch on the right needle.

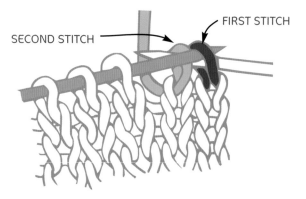

SECOND STITCH

FIRST STITCH

With the left needle, pull this stitch over the second stitch and around the tip of the right needle. (You'll probably notice that the tip of the right needle is hooking the second stitch through the first one.) Now you should have only one stitch on the right needle.

SECOND STITCH

FIRST STITCH (NOW BOUND OFF)

Step 3:
Knit another stitch onto the right needle (don't forget to make the stitches loose enough so you can work them easily). Repeat step 2. Continue this process until there's only one stitch left on your needle.

LOCKING THE BIND OFF

Pull on the remaining stitch on the needle to make a very loose loop and slip it off the needle. Cut the working yarn, leaving an end. Bring the end through the loop, and pull it tight.

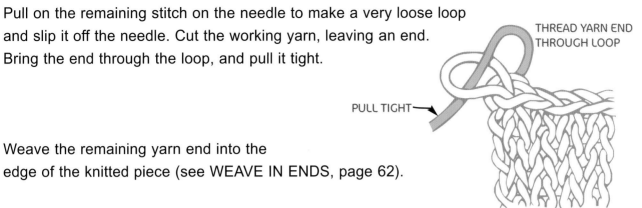

THREAD YARN END
THROUGH LOOP

PULL TIGHT

Weave the remaining yarn end into the edge of the knitted piece (see WEAVE IN ENDS, page 62).

PURL BIND OFF *(use this when the last row of stitches on the needle are purl stitches)*

Step 1:
Purl two stitches.

Step 2:
Insert the left needle into the front of the first purled stitch.

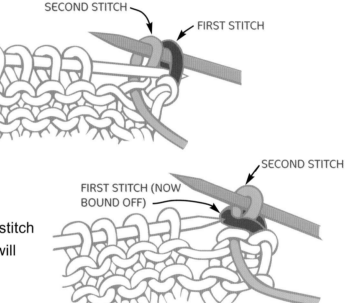

SECOND STITCH
FIRST STITCH

FIRST STITCH (NOW BOUND OFF)
SECOND STITCH

Pull the first stitch over the second stitch and slide it off the left needle. You will have one stitch on the right needle.

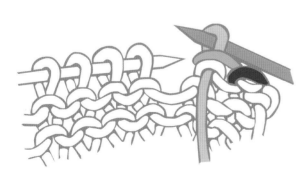

Step 3:
Purl another stitch; repeat step 2.

Continue this process until there's only one stitch left on your needle.

Now you can lock the bind off in the same way you did for the knitted stitches (see LOCKING THE BIND OFF, this page).

HELP!
WHAT IF I WAS KNITTING AND PURLING IN THE SAME ROW?

The bind-off instructions seem easy enough when you're knitting or purling down one whole row. But what do you do if a pattern called for knit and purl stitches in the same row? Do you knit or purl the bind-off?

In cases like this, you follow the pattern. Let's say your last row called for knitting two stitches and then purling two stitches down the row and you have just finished doing that.

1. To bind off, knit two stitches onto the right needle and bind off the first stitch as you would normally bind off a knit stitch (page 16).

2. Now, position your working yarn to purl (bring it in front of the piece). Purl one stitch. Next, using the purl bind off (page 17), bind off the first stitch on your right needle. Purl the second stitch. Then purl bind off the first stitch again.

3. Now, reposition your yarn so that you can knit again. Knit one stitch; then knit bind off one. Knit your second stitch and knit bind off one.

4. Reposition the yarn again to start purling. Purl one stitch; purl bind off the first stitch on the right needle. Purl your second stitch and purl bind off one.

Beginning to detect a pattern? Continue alternating until your row is bound off.

Oops! Too Few Stitches? Not Enough?

DROPPED STITCHES

Let's say you cast on 20 stitches, but after knitting a few rows, suddenly there are only 19 on the needle. You've "dropped" a stitch (it slipped off the needle). Even an experienced knitter drops a stitch from time to time. Don't worry, it's super-easy to fix the mistake.

If the dropped stitch (look for a loop of unknit yarn) is in the row you're working on, or the one just before it, "unknit" your knitting until you get back to the dropped stitch. If the dropped stitch is farther back, see page 20.

To unknit a knit stitch:

1. Hold the knitted piece in your right hand and insert the left needle into the loop just below the stitch to be unknit.

PULL

2. Move this loop from the right onto the left needle. The stitch to be unknit will slide off the right needle. Then, pull the working yarn to pull out the stitch.

3. Continue unknitting until you reach the dropped stitch. Place it back on the left needle (a crochet hook is handy for picking up the stitch). Then, just continue knitting.

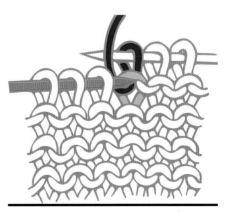

To unknit a purl stitch:

Insert the left needle as described in step 1, picking up the loop just below the stitch to be unknit. This time, be sure to insert the left needle in front of the right one. Then follow steps 2 and 3.

Dropped Stitches Several Rows Back

What if you dropped a stitch several rows back and didn't realize it? You'll notice a gap with lines of unknit yarn. You don't want to unravel all that knitting ... and you don't have to!

1. Slip a crochet hook through the dropped stitch and grab the first line of yarn above the dropped stitch.

DROPPED STITCH

2. Once you have the yarn snagged, pull it forward through the dropped stitch to create a loop.

LINE OF YARN

DROPPED STITCH

3. Now grab the next line of yarn with the crochet hook. As shown above, pull the line of unknit yarn forward, through the new loop, to create yet another loop.

4. Grab each line of yarn following these steps until you've made a loop with the top line of yarn. Now, slide this loop onto the left-hand needle. You're ready to continue knitting!

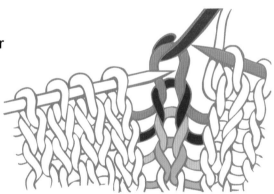

EXTRA STITCHES

What about the opposite problem? It's easy to create an extra stitch accidentally by inserting the right-hand needle not in the top stitch but in the piece of yarn right under it. So instead of the 30 stitches you cast on, suddenly you have 31!

The best way to eliminate the extra stitch is to "knit 2 together" at the end of the row (see DECREASING, page 60).

HOW TO READ A KNITTING PATTERN

The instructions for stitch combinations, called patterns, usually appear between asterisks (*) in a kind of "shorthand." Take a look at the following instructions:

> **Row 1:** Knit 2, *Knit 2, Purl 1, Knit 2 together*; repeat *3 times, Knit 2
>
> **Row 2:** Purl across

This is what those directions mean:

Row 1: First, knit two stitches. Next, knit two stitches, purl one stitch, and then knit two stitches together. Repeat this three-part combination three times. Finally, knit two more stitches.

Row 2: Purl across the row.

It will get easier!

Does it feel really awkward or are you getting confused? Think about each step and don't try to go too fast. With a little time, you won't believe how easy it becomes!

Start at the beginning again, remembering that in the illustrations the working yarn is colored.

Illustrations aren't helpful? Maybe you aren't a visual person, so try just following the words. Or, if the words are confusing you, try just following the illustrations.

If all else fails, ask for help. Knitters love to share what they know!

LOOK FOR THESE ICONS WITH EACH PROJECT:

1

These projects use one stitch and have a very simple pattern to follow.

2

These projects require one or more of the following:

- using two stitches (knit and purl)
- keeping track of many stitches on your needles
- increasing or decreasing stitches
- sewing sections together to complete the piece

3

These projects require ALL of the following:

- using two stitches (knit and purl)
- keeping track of many stitches on your needles
- increasing or decreasing stitches
- sewing sections together to complete the piece

From the Neck Up: Scarves, Headbands & Hats

They're **thick**, they're thin, they're __HOT__, they're IN!
Scarves have burst on to the fashion scene in a big way,
and the days when only people who lived in cold climates
wore knitted scarves are long gone! With the new fun (and
lightweight) yarns, these items are now fashion accessories,
so the more you own, the better. Of course, if you do live
where winters are chilly, these items will keep you cozy too!

Hand-knitted hats and headbands can also reflect your
personal style and your different moods — the playful, fun-
loving side or the bold fashion-statement side. As with all
our knitted creations, you can add your own personal
touches, from buttons and beads to flowers and fur, to the
basic design. Just don't be surprised if your creations start
new trends and family and friends ask you to make some
for them!

SPARKLY SCARF

Scarves are just about the easiest items to knit — you can make lots of different ones even if you only know one stitch! And then you have the fun of customizing them with beads, tassels, fringe, even pockets. But watch out! Once you've finished one scarf, you'll want to start another. That's when you'll know you've been bitten by the knitting bug.

If you find knitting with double strands a little challenging, try knitting with just a strand of the snowdrop yarn until you're a more experienced knitter.

Materials
Knitting needles, size 11
*Eyelash yarn, 1¾ oz/50 g ball, 2
*Snowdrop yarn, 1¾ oz/50 g ball, 2
*Ruler or tape measure
*Scissors
*Yarn needle

Start Knitting!

1.
Using a strand of each yarn (see KNITTING WITH DOUBLE STRANDS, page 25), cast on 13 stitches.

2.
Knit every row until your scarf is as long as you want it to be. When you finish a ball of yarn, start a new one (see ATTACHING A NEW WORKING YARN, page 60).

All I need to know is ...
casting on (page 10)
knit stitch (page 12)
binding off (page 16)

3.
Bind off all stitches, leaving a 4" (10 cm) yarn end.

4.
Using the yarn needle, weave in all loose yarn ends (see WEAVE IN ENDS, page 62).

Fabulous Finishes!

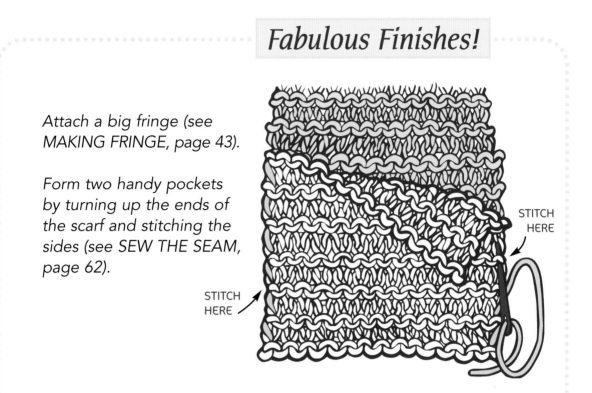

Attach a big fringe (see MAKING FRINGE, page 43).

Form two handy pockets by turning up the ends of the scarf and stitching the sides (see SEW THE SEAM, page 62).

STITCH HERE

STITCH HERE

KNITTING WITH DOUBLE STRANDS

Take a strand of yarn from two different balls and work with them as if they were one strand, holding them together as you knit your piece. Doubling up the yarn creates a sturdy finished piece – great for items like scarves that will get a lot of wear.

More Quick Starts Knitting Fun!

Skinny Scarf

This scarf is finished in a flash because it's so, well, skinny! Wear it as a scarf, wear it as a belt … the point is, just wear it!

Follow the instructions for the SPARKLY SCARF, page 24, but this time:

- ⋆ use size 9 needles

- ⋆ knit with eyelash yarn (1¾ oz/50 g ball) and inchworm yarn (3½ oz/100 g ball)

- ⋆ cast on only 6 stitches

- ⋆ Use a yarn needle and beading thread (available at craft stores) or lightweight yarn to attach beads to each end of the scarf as shown.

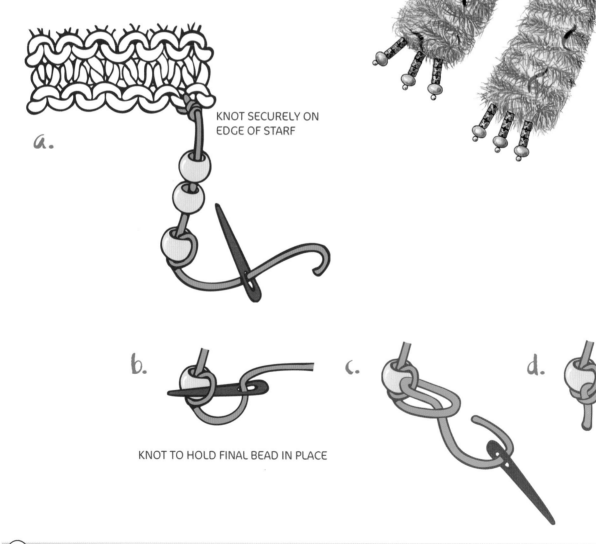

a.

KNOT SECURELY ON EDGE OF STARF

b.

KNOT TO HOLD FINAL BEAD IN PLACE

c.

d.

EAR-WARMING HEADBAND

You probably have more than one coat or jacket, so you need more than one headband, don't you think? You could go out and buy headbands in every color, why not make your own to get exactly the look you want? They'll be cuter, warmer, and way more fun to show off. If you have trouble knitting smoothly with double strands of yarn, try making the headband using just a strand of the popcorn yarn. Or use super bulky weight yarn, which is really easy to work with (and warm too!).

Materials
*Knitting needles, size 10½
*Popcorn yarn, 1¾ oz/50 g ball
*Eyelash yarn, 1¾ oz/50 g ball
*Ruler or tape measure
*Scissors
*Yarn needle
*Decorations (optional): scraps of wool fabric or felt, a button, sewing needle and thread

Start Knitting!

All I need to know is ...

casting on (page 10)
knit stitch (page 12)
binding off (page 16)

1.
Using a strand of each yarn (see KNITTING WITH DOUBLE STRANDS, page 25), cast on 13 stitches.

2.
Knit each row until the piece measures 20" (50 cm) or until it almost fits around your head — leave about a 1" (2.5 cm) gap. If the headband is too long, it won't fit snugly around your head.

3.
Bind off all stitches, leaving a 9" (22.5 cm) yarn end to sew the two ends of the headband together.

4.

Thread the yarn needle with the yarn end and sew the ends of the headband together (see SEW THE SEAM, page 62).

5.

While the needle is still threaded, go in and out with it along the seam. Pull the yarn tight, pinching the seam to gather it slightly as shown in the finished headband. Knot the yarn securely and cut it, leaving a 4" (10 cm) yarn end.

6.

Using the yarn needle, weave in all loose yarn ends (see WEAVE IN ENDS, page 62).

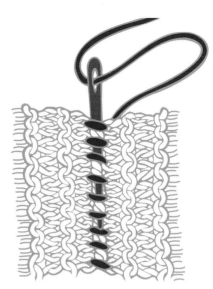

PULL NEEDLE THROUGH TO GATHER

Fabulous Finishes!

Now it's time to take a simply simple headband and turn it into a simply wonderful headband!

To create the tassel shown on page 27, cut several 7" to 9" (17.5 to 22.5 cm) strands of the eyelash yarn. Wrap one around the pinched area and knot it. Repeat with remaining strands. Cut to desired length.

Cut the scrap of wool fabric or felt in the shape of a flower blossom. Make a second, slightly smaller one. Place the blossoms together on the headband and sew a button in the center.

JAZZY BEADED HAIR BAND

Quick and oh-so-easy to make, a hair band is a great way to use up a leftover bit of a favorite yarn. We used worsted-weight yarn here because it's so easy to work with. Or try a mohair-look yarn, which would make a nice soft hair band. In fact, why not make lots of hair bands in all your favorite colors and yarn types?

Materials

*Knitting needles, size 8
*Worsted-weight yarn, small ball left over from another project
*Ruler or tape measure
*Scissors
*Yarn needle
*Decorations (optional): special pin, beads, or a wool flower (see page 28)

Start knitting!

1.
Cast on 10 stitches.

2.
Work in the following pattern:
   ROW 1: *Knit 2, Purl 2*; repeat * to end of row.
   (See HOW TO READ A KNITTING PATTERN, page 21.)
   ROW 2: *Purl 2, Knit 2*; repeat * to end of row.

All I need to know is ...

casting on (page 10)
knit stitch (page 12)
purl stitch (page 14)
binding off (page 16)

3.

Repeat rows 1 and 2 until the headband measures 20" (50 cm) or until it almost fits around your head; leave a 1" (2.5 cm) gap between the ends for a snug fit.

4.

To finish, follow steps 3 through 6 from the EAR-WARMING HEADBAND on pages 27 to 28.

Fabulous Finishes!

Here are some ways to make this project uniquely yours. We're sure you can think of others!

• Accessorize your hair band with beads (as we did) by attaching them with beading thread as shown. Knot the thread securely on the back side.

• Add a wool or felt flower (see page 28).

• Attach a fun sparkly pin.

TWIST & TWINKLE TASSEL HAT

The beaded stars really do twinkle when the light hits them — you're going to love it!

Materials
* Knitting needles, size 13
* Super bulky weight yarn, 6 oz/170 g ball, 2
* Ruler or tape measure
* Scissors
* Yarn needle
* Beads (we used 12 mm stars)

Start knitting!

Make the hat

1.
Cast on 50 stitches for a 20"-diameter (50 cm) hat.

2.
Work in the following pattern until the hat measures 7" (17.5 cm):

ROW 1: * Knit 1, Purl 1 *; repeat * to the end of the row (see HOW TO READ A KNITTING PATTERN, page 21).
ROW 2: * Purl 1, Knit 1 *; repeat * to the end of the row.

When you finish a ball of yarn, start a new one (see ATTACHING A NEW WORKING YARN, page 60).

All I need to know is ...
casting on (page 10)
knit stitch (page 12)
purl stitch (page 14)

Begin decreasing (see DECREASING, page 60)

3.

Knit 2 together, repeat * to the end of the row (at the end, 25 stitches will remain on the needle).

4.

Purl 2 together, repeat * to the end of the row, purl remaining stitch (13 stitches remain on the needle).

5.

Knit 2 together, repeat * to the end of the row, knit remaining stitch (7 stitches remain on the needle).

Quick Starts Tips!™

Reminder: Count those stitches!

When you're knitting a piece that has a lot of stitches (50, in this case), it's a good idea to count them every few rows. If you find you've dropped a stitch, see pages 19 to 20 for a fast and easy repair!

THREADED YARN NEEDLE
YARN CUT FROM BALL

6.

Cut the yarn, leaving a 15" to 18" (37.5 to 45 cm) yarn end to sew the hat seam later.

7.

Thread the yarn end onto the yarn needle and slip it through the stitches remaining on the knitting needle. Pull out the knitting needle. Pull the yarn to close the opening.

8.

With the yarn needle still threaded, sew the two edges together (see SEW THE SEAM, page 62) to form the hat. Knot the yarn and cut it, leaving a 4" (10 cm) end.

9.

Using the yarn needle, weave in all loose yarn ends (see WEAVE IN ENDS, page 62).

Turn the hat right side out.

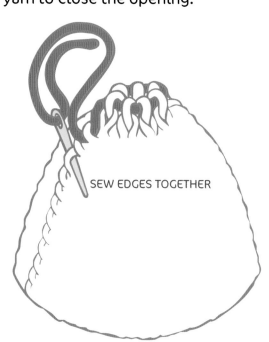

SEW EDGES TOGETHER

Make the tassels

1.

Cut 20 pieces of the yarn (more or less, depending on how many tassels you want) approximately 9" (22.5 cm) long.

2.

From the outside of the hat, attach each tassel as shown. Use a crochet hook to pull the yarn piece through the stitches, if that's easier.

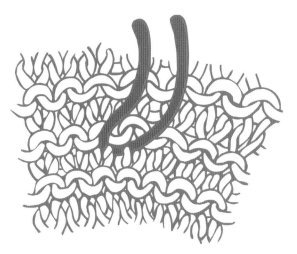

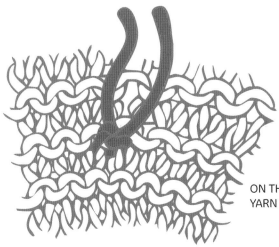

PUSH ONE END OF THE YARN PIECE UNDER A STITCH AND OUT THE OTHER SIDE. PULL THE YARN PIECE THROUGH UNTIL THE ENDS ARE EVEN.

ON THE OUTSIDE OF THE HAT, KNOT THE YARN TO SECURE THE TASSEL IN PLACE.

3.

Repeat step 2 until you've used up all the yarn pieces.

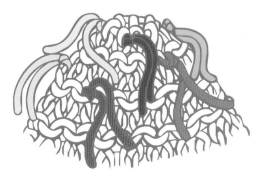

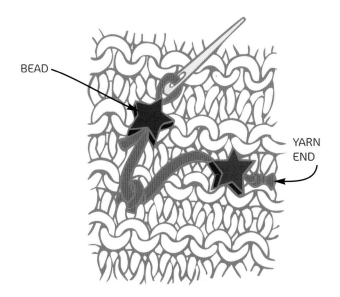

BEAD

YARN END

4.

Thread the yarn needle with one yarn end. Pull the needle through a bead so it slips onto the yarn. Knot the yarn end so the bead won't slide off.

Repeat until there are beads on all the yarn ends.

POM-POM HAT

The more "poms" on this hat, the better! Now, we'll mention right off, 65 stitches is a lot to keep track of if you're a beginner, so just be sure to stop and count them every now and then. If you've dropped one (or picked up an extra), go right to pages 19 to 20 to see how to fix it.

If knitting with double strands of yarn is a little challenging, just use a single strand of the eyelash yarn. And if you want a simpler project where you can practice knitting with double strands of yarn, try the SPARKLY SCARF (pages 24 to 26) or the EAR-WARMING HEADBAND (pages 27 to 28).

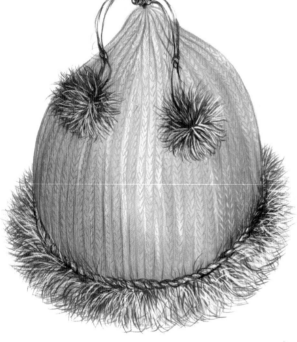

Materials
* **Knitting needles, size 9**
* **Eyelash yarn, 1¾ oz/50 g ball rolled into 2 balls (see page 8)**
* **Ruler or tape measure**
* **Scissors**
* **Mohair-look yarn, 3 oz/85 g ball**
* **Yarn needle**

Start knitting!

~~~~~~~⟶ *Make the hat*

All I need to know is ...

casting on (page 10)
knit stitch (page 12)
purl stitch (page 14)

1.

Using double strands (see KNITTING WITH DOUBLE STRANDS, page 25) of the eyelash yarn, cast on 65 stitches for a 20"-diameter (50 cm) hat.

2.

Knit 8 rows.

3.

Cut the yarns, leaving 4" (10 cm) ends to weave in later.

4.

Attach the mohair-look yarn (see ATTACH-ING A NEW WORKING YARN, page 60).

5.

Knit a row, then purl a row until the hat measures 6"/15 cm (5"/12.5 cm small; 7"/17.5 cm large) from the cast-on edge.

Begin decreasing (see DECREASING, page 60):

6.

Knit 6, Knit 2 together; repeat * to end of row, knit remaining stitch (see HOW TO READ A KNITTING PATTERN, page 21).

7.

Purl a row.

8.

*Knit 5, Knit 2 together *; repeat * to end of row, knit remaining stitch.

9.

Purl a row.

10.

Knit 4, Knit 2 together; repeat * to end of row, knit remaining stitch.

11.

Purl a row.

12.

*Knit 3, Knit 2 together *; repeat * to end of row, knit remaining stitch.

13.

Purl a row.

14.

Repeat rows 12 and 13 (knitting any remaining stitches in the repeats) until there are 12 stitches left on the needle.

15.

Cut the yarn, leaving a 15" to 18" (37.5 to 45 cm) yarn end to sew the hat seam.

16.

Thread the yarn needle with the yarn end and pull through the 12 stitches on the knitting needle.

Slide the stitches off the knitting needle. Pull to close the opening and form the hat.

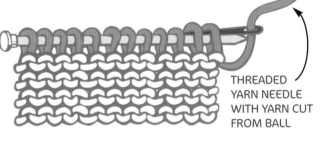

THREADED YARN NEEDLE WITH YARN CUT FROM BALL

PULL

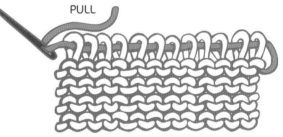

17.

With the yarn still threaded on the needle, sew the two edges of the hat together (see SEW THE SEAM, page 62). Knot the yarn and cut it, leaving a 4" (10 cm) yarn end.

18.

Using the yarn needle, weave in all loose yarn ends (see WEAVE IN ENDS, page 62).

Turn the hat right side out.

 *Make the pom-poms (make 2)*

1.

With the eyelash yarn and the size 9 needles, cast on 10 stitches.

2.

Knit 10 rows.

3.

Bind off all stitches. Cut the yarn, leaving a 12" (30 cm) end, and thread it through the yarn needle.

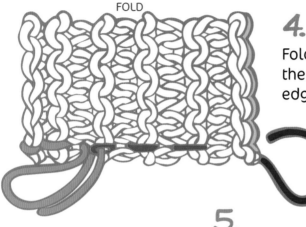
FOLD

4.

Fold the piece in half as shown. Weave the needle in and out along the bottom edge (leaving the side edges open).

5.

Remove the yarn needle. Pull the yarn ends tightly to gather the stitches, creating the pom-pom. Knot the two yarn ends tightly.

6.

Push the yarn ends through the top of the hat and knot them on the inside, leaving some of the yarn on the outside so your poms will swing and sway as you walk and talk.

THE FUN OF USING EYELASH YARN IS HOW THE "SQUARE" YOU KNITTED POOFS OUT INTO A BIG FUZZY POM-POM!

More Quick Starts Knitting Fun!

Make as many pom-poms as you like. If you have a few balls of fuzzy yarns in different colors, they would look great mixed in on top of your hat.

Knits for All Seasons!

Did you ever imagine knitting a summer garment? Sounds like a contradiction, doesn't it? But there's a wide world of fun-to-wear items you can knit to carry you through all four seasons. Using cotton or acrylic-blend yarns, you can make yourself a "hot" halter top, for example, that's comfortably cool to wear.

We're always amazed by how fashion trends come and go … and then come back again! Ponchos are back, but this time with a fresh new look. Gone are the stiff, bulky materials of yesterday, replaced by soft textures and a wide array of color choices. With these lightweight yarns, you can make ponchos that are part of your outfit as well as cool-weather wraps.

And don't forget mittens! Your bureau drawer is filled with lots of colorful socks, isn't it? So don't neglect your hands! Find a basket and fill it with brightly colored mittens that *you* knitted. Like socks, you can never have too many! They're handy to have for those cool mornings or give as gifts to friends and family.

"HOT" HALTER TOP

This halter top is hot — it's cool to wear when it's hot and it's hot because it's so cool! Got it?

The halter has a lot of stitches to keep track of, especially if you're making the large size, so be sure to count the number of stitches on your needle every now and then. To fix dropped or extra stitches, see pages 19 to 20.

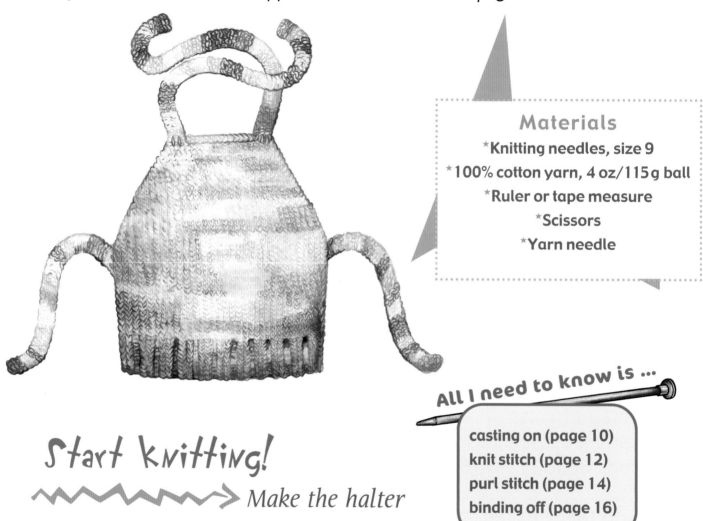

Materials
*Knitting needles, size 9
*100% cotton yarn, 4 oz/115g ball
*Ruler or tape measure
*Scissors
*Yarn needle

All I need to know is ...

casting on (page 10)
knit stitch (page 12)
purl stitch (page 14)
binding off (page 16)

Start Knitting!

→ *Make the halter*

1.
Cast on 72 stitches for small (84 stitches for medium, 94 stitches for large).

2.
Knit 2, Purl 2; repeat * to end of row (see HOW TO READ A KNITTING PATTERN, page 21). Repeat rows until piece measures 2" (5 cm) to form the ribbed bottom edge.

3.
Knit a row, then purl a row until the halter measures 5"/12.5 cm (5"/12.5 cm medium; 6"/15 cm large). from the cast-on edge; stop after working a purl row.

Begin decreasing each side
(see DECREASING, pages 60 to 61):

4.

On the next row, knit 1, knit 2 together, then knit the row until there are 3 stitches remaining on the needle. To decrease this time, you're going to slip stitch, pass slip stitch over: slip 1, knit 1, pass slip stitch over, knit 1.

5.

Purl a row.

6.

Repeat steps 4 and 5 until there are 28 stitches (34 for medium, 40 for large) remaining on the needle. The halter top now looks like this.

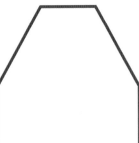

7.

Bind off all stitches, leaving a 4" (10 cm) yarn end.

8.

Using the yarn needle, weave in all loose yarn ends (see WEAVE IN ENDS, page 62).

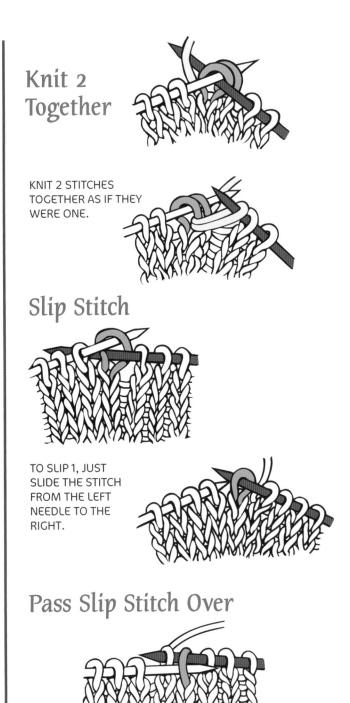

Knit 2 Together

KNIT 2 STITCHES TOGETHER AS IF THEY WERE ONE.

Slip Stitch

TO SLIP 1, JUST SLIDE THE STITCH FROM THE LEFT NEEDLE TO THE RIGHT.

Pass Slip Stitch Over

LIFT THE SLIPPED STITCH OVER THE NEXT KNITTED STITCH.

SIZING YOUR HALTER TOP

	Small (6–8)	Medium (10–12)	Large (14–16)
width at cast-on edge:	14" (35 cm)	17" (42.5 cm)	20" (50 cm)
width at bound-off edge	7" (17.5 cm)	8½" (21 cm)	10" (25 cm)
overall length	13" (32.5 cm)	14½" (36 cm)	16" (40 cm)

Make the halter ties

9.

With the knit side facing you (see KNIT SIDE? PURL SIDE?, page 46), slip a knitting needle into 3 stitches on one end of the bound-off edge of the halter top. Knot the strand from the yarn ball onto the last stitch you picked up.

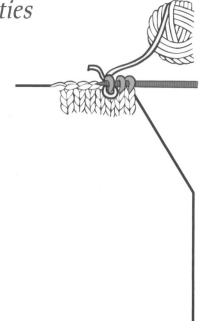

10.

Knit until the halter tie is 12" (30 cm) long (or longer if necessary to fit you comfortably). Bind off, leaving a 4" (10 cm) yarn end.

11.

Repeat steps 9 and 10 on the other side of the bound-off top.

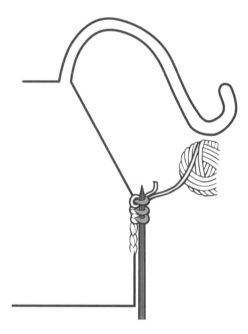

12.

Pick up 3 stitches on one side of the halter as shown and knot the strand from the yarn ball onto the last stitch you picked up. Knit a tie 12" (30 cm) long. Bind off all stitches, leaving a 4" (10 cm) yarn end.

13.

Repeat step 12 on the other side of the halter.

14.

Using the yarn needle, weave in all loose yarn ends (see WEAVE IN ENDS, page 62).

More Quick Starts Knitting Fun!

Double the yarn (see KNITTING WITH DOUBLE STRANDS, page 25) to create a thicker halter top. Try using a strand of cotton with a strand of your favorite novelty yarn for an eye-popping style!

POPULAR PONCHO

How do knitted rectangles turn into a stylish poncho? It's easy — you'll see! Larger-sized needles (sizes 13–17) and fine yarn will give this poncho a lacy look; using smaller-sized needles (sizes 9–11) and thicker yarn will add weight and warmth, so it's more like a sweater.

Materials

Knitting needles, size 11

*Mohair-look yarn, 3 oz/85g ball, 6

*Eyelash yarn, 1¾ oz/50g ball, 8

*Ruler or tape measure

*Scissors

*Yarn needle

*To make fringe (optional): cardboard, leftover yarn from poncho, crochet hook

Start knitting!

Knit the front and back pieces

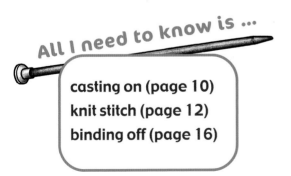

All I need to know is ...

casting on (page 10)

knit stitch (page 12)

binding off (page 16)

1.

Working with one strand each of mohair-look and eyelash yarns (see WORKING WITH DOUBLE STRANDS, page 25), cast on 20 stitches (small, size 6–8) or 30 stitches (medium, size 10–12) or 40 stitches (large, size 14–16).

2.

Knit every row until the piece measures 32" (80 cm). (To attach a new working yarn, see page 60.)

3.

Bind off all stitches, leaving a 4" (10 cm) yarn end.

4.

Using the yarn needle, weave in all loose yarn ends (see WEAVE IN ENDS, page 62).

5.

Repeat steps 1 through 4 to make a second rectangle.

Sew the poncho together

1.

Place the two pieces as shown. Using the yarn needle and a strand of either yarn, sew together where indicated (see SEW THE SEAM, page 62). Knot the yarn and cut it, leaving a 4" (10 cm) end.

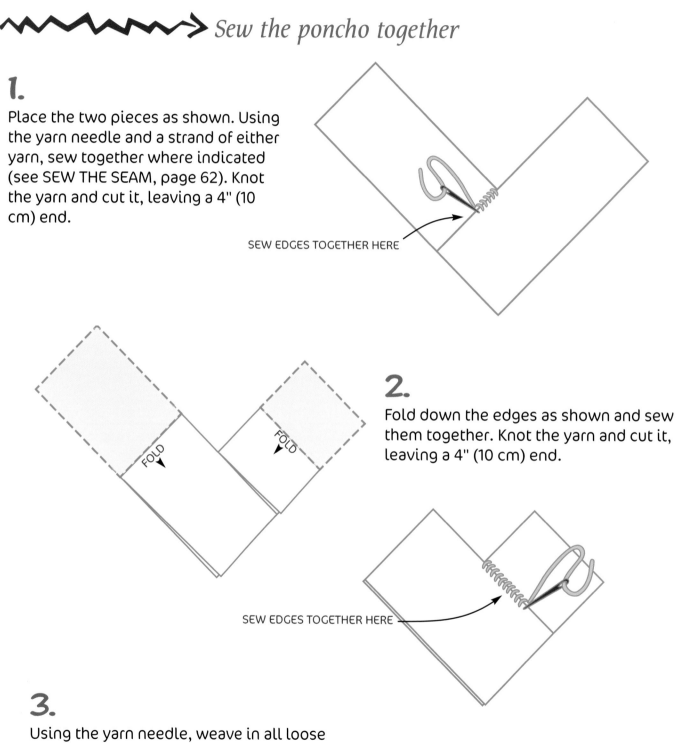

SEW EDGES TOGETHER HERE

FOLD

FOLD

2.

Fold down the edges as shown and sew them together. Knot the yarn and cut it, leaving a 4" (10 cm) end.

SEW EDGES TOGETHER HERE

3.

Using the yarn needle, weave in all loose yarn ends (see WEAVE IN ENDS, page 62).

*Accessorize with a cluster of flowers from the craft store, some fun buttons, or a large pin.

*Add fringe along the outside edges (as shown below).

MAKING FRINGE

1. Cut a rectangle out of cardboard. We suggest 5" x 12" (12.5 x 30 cm), but the first measurement determines how long the fringe will be, so adjust the size according to what you would like. Loosely wind the yarn around the cardboard several times. Cut the yarn across one end.

2. Repeat step 1 until you have the desired amount of fringe (you can always make more if you run out!).

3. Take two strands of the cut yarn and fold them in half. Using a crochet hook, draw the folded ends through one of the bound-off stitches on the edge where you want the fringe.

Pull the loose ends through the folded end.

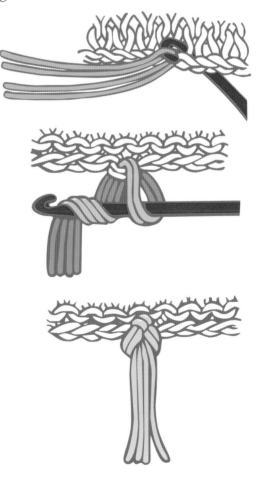

4. Pull the loose ends tightly to form a knot. Repeat this step until you have evenly spaced sets of fringe around the poncho.

5. Lay the poncho on a table. Trim the fringe ends so they are even.

MIGHTY FINE MITTENS

We love to whip up a pair of mittens to match a new coat or to give to someone as a gift on a cold winter day. They're real attention-grabbers, especially when you use bright colors. Whether they're solid or striped, have cozy ribbed cuffs or eye-catching fuzzy ones (see page 48), your mittens will make a statement — one that says, "I'm warm, I'm happy, and I'm ready to go!"

Materials
*Knitting needles, size 10
*Super bulky weight yarn,
6 oz/170 g ball, 2
*Ruler or tape measure
*Stitch holders, 2
*Scissors
*Yarn needle

Start Knitting!
To make one mitten

All I need to know is ...

casting on (page 10)
knit stitch (page 12)
purl stitch (page 14)

1.
Cast on 21 stitches.

2.
Knit 1, Purl 1; repeat * to the end of the row (see HOW TO READ A KNITTING PATTERN, page 21). Repeat this pattern until the piece measures 3"/7.5 cm to form the ribbed cuff.

3.
Knit a row.

4.
Purl a row.

5.
Knit a row.

6.
Purl a row.

7

Increase to start the thumb (see INCREASING, page 61)

Row 1: Knit 10 stitches, increase 1, knit 1, increase 1, knit 10 (you now have 23 stitches on the needle).

Row 2: Purl a row.

Row 3: Knit 10, increase 1, knit 3, increase 1, knit 10 (25 stitches now on needle).

Row 4: Purl a row.

Row 5: Knit 10, increase 1, knit 5, increase 1, knit 10 (27 stitches on needle).

Row 6: Purl a row.

Knit the thumb

Knit Increase

INSERT THE RIGHT NEEDLE INTO THE STITCH TO BE INCREASED. KNIT THAT STITCH, BUT DON'T SLIP THE STITCH OFF THE LEFT NEEDLE. PULL THE RIGHT NEEDLE SLIGHTLY TO MAKE A SMALL LOOP.

SWITCH THE POSITION OF YOUR NEEDLES AND INSERT THE RIGHT NEEDLE INTO THE BACK OF THE STITCH STILL ON THE LEFT NEEDLE. KNIT THAT STITCH AGAIN, THIS TIME COMPLETING IT.

8.

Step 1: Knit 10 stitches; slide those stitches onto one of the stitch holders.

Step 2: Knit the next 7 stitches.

Step 3: Slide the remaining 10 stitches onto the other stitch holder (don't knit these 10 stitches yet).

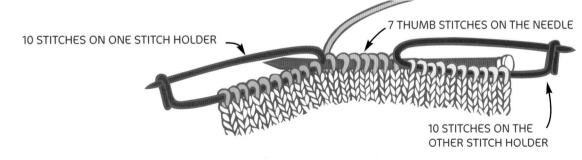

10 STITCHES ON ONE STITCH HOLDER

7 THUMB STITCHES ON THE NEEDLE

10 STITCHES ON THE OTHER STITCH HOLDER

9.

Working with the 7 stitches on the knitting needle only, purl 1 row, knit 1 row, purl 1 row, knit 1 row, and purl 1 row (you've just completed 5 rows) to make the thumb. When you finish a ball of yarn, start a new one (see ATTACHING A NEW WORKING YARN, page 60).

10.

Decrease the thumb piece (see DECREASING, page 60)

Row 1: Knit 1, knit 2 together, knit 1, knit 2 together, knit 1 (5 stitches now on the needle).

Row 2: Purl 1, purl 2 together, purl 2.

Row 3: Knit 4.

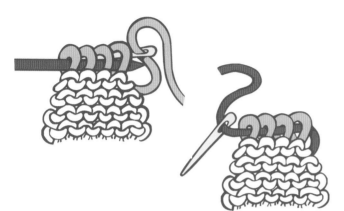

11.

With the purl side facing you, cut the yarn, leaving a 10" (25 cm) end to sew the thumb seam. Thread the yarn end onto the yarn needle and pull it through the remaining stitches on the knitting needle. Slide the stitches off the needle. Pull yarn to close opening.

12.

With the yarn still on the yarn needle, sew the thumb seam (see SEW THE SEAM, page 62). When you finish, the thumb will be inside out (purl side out). Knot the yarn and cut it, leaving a 4" (10 cm) yarn end.

Finish knitting the mitten

13.

With the knit side facing you, hold one knitting needle in your right hand and slip the stitches from the stitch holder on the right side onto it.

Quick Starts Tips!™

Knit side? Purl side?

Here's how to tell them apart!

KNIT SIDE   PURL SIDE

14.

Pick up 2 stitches from the base of the thumb (at the place where you finished sewing the thumb seam) by slipping the point of the knitting needle into them.

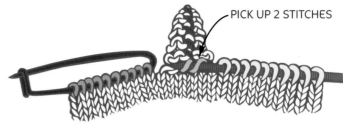

PICK UP 2 STITCHES

15.

Attach the working yarn to the last stitch picked up at the base of the thumb (see ATTACHING A NEW WORKING YARN, page 60).

16.

Hold the second knitting needle in your left hand and slip the stitches from the second stitch holder onto it. Knit the remainder of the row you began in step 8.

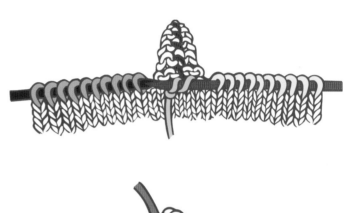

17.

Knit a row, then purl a row. Continue knitting and purling by rows until the mitten measures 3" (7.5 cm) from the base of the thumb, ending with a purl row.

Begin decreasing (see DECREASING, page 60)

18.

Knit 2, Knit 2 together; repeat * to end of row, knit 2 remaining stitches.

19.

Purl a row.

20.

Knit 1, Knit 2 together; repeat * to end of row, knit 2 remaining stitches.

21.

Purl a row.

22.

Knit 1, Knit 2 together; repeat * to end of row.

23.

Purl a row.

24.

Cut the yarn, leaving a 15" (37.5 cm) yarn end to sew the mitten side seam (see SEW THE SEAM, page 62).

25.

Thread the yarn end onto the yarn needle and pull it through the remaining stitches on the knitting needle as shown in step 11; pull to tighten the opening.

26.

Sew the two edges of the mitten together (see SEW THE SEAM, page 62). The mitten will be purl side out. Knot the yarn and cut it, leaving a 4" (10 cm) end.

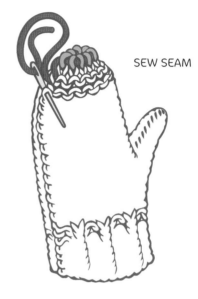

SEW SEAM

27.

Using the yarn needle, weave in all loose yarn ends (see WEAVE IN ENDS, page 62).

Turn the mitten right side (knit side) out.

28.

Repeat all the steps to make the second mitten.

More Quick Starts Knitting Fun!

Add a fuzzy cuff! Starting with size 9 needles, knit the first 3" (7.5 cm) of the mitten with double strands (see KNITTING WITH DOUBLE STRANDS, page 25) of eyelash yarn in the color of your choice. Switch to one strand of multi-colored sport-weight yarn (see ATTACHING A NEW WORKING YARN, page 60).

More Knitted Creations!

OK, so you love to knit things that you can wear, but why stop there? For starters, we're sure you need a handy little hip bag so you can carry along your essentials. These are right in style (and this project is especially fun because you get to try a technique called felting).

Or, how about some hand-knitted fashion statements for a canine friend? How about matching kerchiefs for you and your dog? And wouldn't it be fun to knit a doggy sweater, especially when you make the poncho on page 41 in the same yarn for yourself? The next time you take your dog for a walk on a chilly day, he'll thank you for the added warmth. If you don't have a dog of your own, make one for a friend who does. It's like giving a pooch a knitted hug!

FELTED HIP BAG

This cute little bag only looks hard because you use several different types and colors of yarn — it's easy to knit! For the perfect finishing touch, felt it (page 53) to make it sturdy and strong.

Materials
*Knitting needles, size 15
*Eyelash yarn, 1 ball or some left over from another project
*Sport-weight yarn, 1 ball or some left from another project
*Ruler or tape measure
*Scissors
*Metallic-blend yarn, 1 ball rolled into 2 balls
*100% wool yarn (any animal fiber), 5 oz/140 g ball
*Yarn needle
*Double-pointed knitting needles, size 6
*Decorations (optional): beads, buttons, bows, bangles or old earrings that have lost their mates; ribbon; sewing needle and thread

Start Knitting!

〰〰〰〰➤ *Make the bag*

All I need to know is ...
casting on (page 10)
knit stitch (page 12)
binding off (page 16)

1.
With one strand each of the eyelash and sport-weight yarns (see KNITTING WITH DOUBLE STRANDS, page 25) and the size 15 needles, cast on 48 stitches.

2.
Knit 6 rows.

3.

Cut the yarns, leaving 10" (25 cm) ends (to sew the bag together later).

4.

At the beginning of the next row, attach the two strands of the metallic-blend yarn (see ATTACHING A NEW WORKING YARN, page 60).

5.

Knit 12 rows.

6.

Cut the metallic-blend yarn, leaving 10" (25 cm) ends.

7.

At the beginning of the next row, attach the wool yarn (see step 4).

8.

Knit until the piece measures 17" (42.5 cm) from the cast-on edge.

9.

Bind off all stitches. Cut the yarn, leaving a 18" (45 cm) end.

10.

Fold the bag in half. Thread the yarn needle with the yarn end from step 9 and sew the side and bottom seams (see SEW THE SEAM, page 62) up to the top of the wool yarn section. Knot the yarn and cut it, leaving a 4" (10 cm) end.

11.

Thread the yarn needle with the metallic-yarn ends and sew that section of the side seam. Knot the yarn and cut it, leaving a 4" (10 cm) end.

12.

Repeat step 11 using the eyelash and sport-weight yarn ends to sew the last section of the side seam.

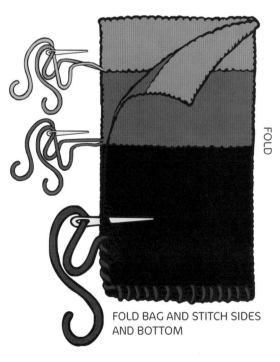

FOLD

FOLD BAG AND STITCH SIDES AND BOTTOM

13.

Using the yarn needle, weave in all loose yarn ends
(see WEAVE IN ENDS, page 62).

 Make the strap

1.

Using the double-pointed needles and
the wool yarn, cast on 5 stitches.

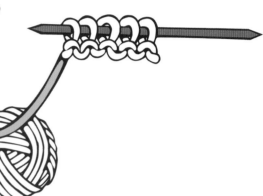

2.

Knit a row.

3.

Without turning the needle
around, slide the stitches to
the other end of the needle.

4.

Bring the working yarn behind the stitches so it's at the other end of
the needle and knit the row. The working yarn passes between the
two needles before you knit the first stitch at the right-hand end of
the needle.

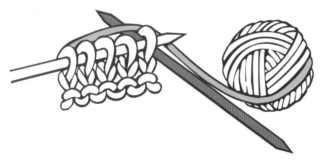 

5.

Repeat steps 3 and 4 until the
strap is about 7' (2 m) long (it will
shrink during the felting process).
As you slide the stitches back and
forth and knit at each end, a slen-
der tube forms.

6.

Bind off the stitches, leaving a 4" (10 cm) yarn end. Sew each end of the strap to the bag (see SEW THE SEAM, page 62). Knot the yarn and cut it, leaving a 4" (10 cm) yarn end.

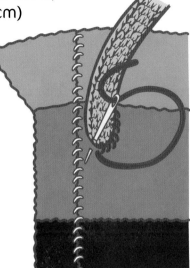

7.

Using the yarn needle, weave in all loose yarn ends (see WEAVE IN ENDS, page 62).

Turn the bag right side out.

Fabulous Finishes!

We trimmed our bag by sewing on a length of beaded ribbon with a running stitch — but you can use whatever inspires you!

RUNNING STITCH

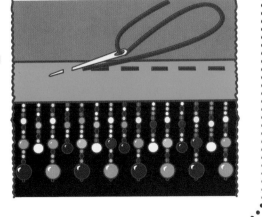

HOW TO FELT

Felting is a technique for treating a hand-knitted item in the washing machine. The finished hip bag will shrink considerably (almost half the knitted size) and the fibers really tighten up, making it very sturdy.

1. Set the washing machine on the "hot" temperature and "low" water level settings. Add a small amount of laundry detergent (1 to 2 tablespoons/15 to 30 ml).

....

2. Place the hip bag inside an old pillowcase and knot loosely. Wash the pillowcase with a couple of bath towels (this will help agitate it evenly).

....

3. Check after 15 minutes or so to see if the bag has shrunk to the size you want; if not, resume washing and check a few minutes later.

....

4. If your bag has shrunk to the desired size before going through the rinse cycle, remove it from the pillowcase and rinse the bag in the sink under cold water, squeezing out all excess water. Otherwise, let it finish the cycle, then remove it from the pillowcase and allow it to air dry, shaping as desired. You may have to "persuade" the item to take on the shape you want, but just stretch, tug, and pull until it's perfect.

CANINE KERCHIEF

Make one for your dog and one for you, too —
how about a matching pair?

Materials

*Knitting needles, size 7
*Sport- or worsted-weight
yarn (cotton for summer,
wool for winter), 1 ball
*Ruler or tape measure
*Scissors
*Yarn needle

All I need to know is ...

casting on (page 10)
knit stitch (page 12)
binding off (page 16)

Start Knitting!

Make the kerchief

1.

Cast on 3 stitches.

Begin increasing (see INCREASING, page 61)

2.

Knit 1 stitch, increase 1, knit 1, increase 1, knit 1.
Now you have 5 stitches on the needle.

3.

Knit a row.

4.

Knit 1, increase 1, knit until there's one stitch remaining, increase 1, knit 1. Now you have 7 stitches on the needle.

5.

Knit a row.

6.

Repeat steps 4 and 5 until the kerchief is the size you want: the more you knit, the bigger the triangle will get. The last row should fit around your dog's neck (or, if it's for you, your head).

7.

Bind off all stitches, leaving a 4" (10 cm) end.

Attach the ties

8.

Cut two 12" (30 cm) strands of yarn for ties. Using the yarn needle, slip one end of each strand through a few stitches at the long ends of the kerchief and knot the yarn to secure it.

9.

Using the yarn needle, weave in all loose yarn ends (see WEAVE IN ENDS, page 62).

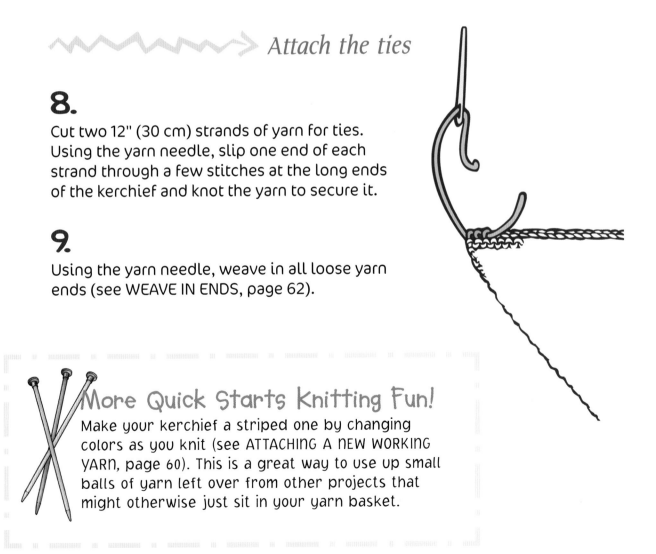

More Quick Starts Knitting Fun!

Make your kerchief a striped one by changing colors as you knit (see ATTACHING A NEW WORKING YARN, page 60). This is a great way to use up small balls of yarn left over from other projects that might otherwise just sit in your yarn basket.

"DOGGY" TURTLENECK SWEATER

The first time you put this sweater on your dog, have a camera ready! You'll want everyone to see how cute your pooch looks in full fashion. This sweater was designed for Bear, who just happens to be our favorite model!

Materials
*Knitting needles, size 10½
*Mohair-look yarn, 3 oz/85 g ball, 3
Ruler or tape measure
*Scissors
*Yarn needle

Start knitting!

〰〰〰➤ Knit the top sweater panel
(covers the back of the dog)

1.

Cast on 48 stitches for a medium-sized dog (40 for a small dog, 60 for a large dog).

All I need to know is ...

casting on (page 10)
knit stitch (page 12)
purl stitch (page 14)
binding off (page 16)

2.

Work in the following stitch pattern until the piece measures 8"/20 cm (6"/15 cm for small; 10"/25 cm for large).

Row 1: *Knit 2, Purl 2*; repeat * to the end of the row (see HOW TO READ A KNITTING PATTERN, page 21).
Row 2: *Purl 2, Knit 2*; repeat * to the end of the row.

Begin decreasing (see DECREASING, page 60)

3.

Knit 2 together, purl 2, *Knit 2, Purl 2*; repeat * until there are 4 stitches remaining on the needle, knit 2, purl 2 together.

4.

Purl 1, knit 2, *Purl 2, Knit 2*; repeat * until 3 stitches remain, purl 2, knit 1.

5.

Knit 1, purl 2 together, *Knit 2, Purl 2*; repeat * until 3 stitches remain, knit 2 together, purl 1.

6.

Purl 1, knit 1, *Purl 2, Knit 2*; repeat * until 2 stitches remain, purl 1, knit 1.

7.

Your pattern of knitting the purl stitches and purling the knit stitches as you go back and forth will change a little at the beginning and end of this row. Just follow the directions and you'll be all set!

Knit 2 together (the first knit stitch and the second purl stitch), *Knit 2, Purl 2*; repeat * until 2 stitches remain, knit 2 together (the first knit stitch and the second purl stitch).

8.

Knit 1, *Purl 2, Knit 2*; repeat * until 1 stitch remains, knit 1. Work in this stitch pattern until the piece measures 17"/42.5 cm (15"/37.5 cm small; 20"/50 cm large).

9.

Bind off all stitches, leaving a 4" (10 cm) end.

10.

Using the yarn needle, weave in all loose yarn ends (see WEAVE IN ENDS, page 62).

Bind-off short cut

The correct way to bind off is to use either the knit bind off or the purl bind off, depending on the stitch on your needle (as the instruction on page 18 indicate). But you're working with a lot of stitches on your needle here, so if you want an easier way, you can use the knit bind off on each stitch. No one will really be able to tell the difference in the finished row!

Knit the bottom sweater panel
(covers the chest and underbelly of the dog)

1.
Cast on 28 stitches for medium (20 for small, 40 for large).

2.
Work in the following stitch pattern until the piece measures 8"/20 cm (6"/15 cm for small; 10"/25 cm for large).

Row 1: *Knit 2, Purl 2*; repeat * to the end of the row.
Row 2: *Purl 2, Knit 2*; repeat * to the end of the row.

Begin decreasing (see DECREASING, page 60)

3.
Knit 2 together, purl 2, *Knit 2, Purl 2*; repeat * until there are 4 stitches remaining on the needle, knit 2, purl 2 together.

4.
Purl 1, knit 2, *Purl 2, Knit 2*; repeat * until 3 stitches remain, purl 2, knit 1.

5.
Knit 1, purl 2 together, *Knit 2, Purl 2*; repeat * until 3 stitches remain, knit 2 together, purl 1.

6.
Purl 1, knit 1, *Purl 2, Knit 2*; repeat * until 2 stitches remain, purl 1, knit 1.

7.
Knit 2 together (the first knit stitch and the second purl stitch), *Knit 2, Purl 2*; repeat * until 2 stitches remain, knit 2 together (the first knit stitch and the second purl stitch).

8.
Knit 1, *Purl 2, Knit 2*; repeat * until 1 stitch remains, knit 1. Work in this stitch pattern until the piece measures 17"/42.5 cm (15"/37.5 cm small; 20"/50 cm large).

9.
Bind off all stitches, leaving a 4" (10 cm) end.

10.
Using the yarn needle, weave in all loose yarn ends (see WEAVE IN ENDS, page 62).

11.

Place the two sweater panels together as shown.

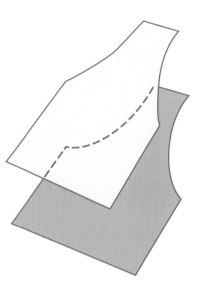

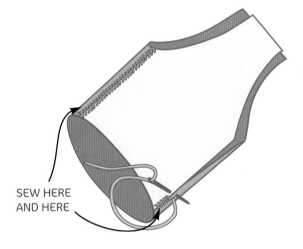

Thread the yarn needle with yarn; sew the two sides from the bottom up to the leg openings or to where you started to decrease (see SEW THE SEAM, page 62). Knot the yarn and cut it, leaving a 4" (10 cm) yarn end.

SEW HERE AND HERE

SEW HERE AND HERE

Thread the needle and sew the neck seams down to the top of the leg openings.

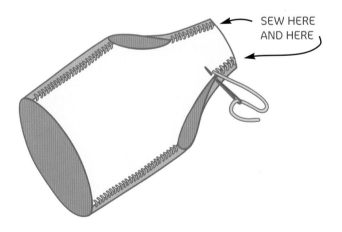

12.

Using the yarn needle, weave in all loose yarn ends (see WEAVE IN ENDS, page 62). Turn the sweater inside out. You're finished! Roll the neck down, slip the sweater on Fido, and head out for a walk!

Quick Starts Illustrated Stitch & How-to Dictionary

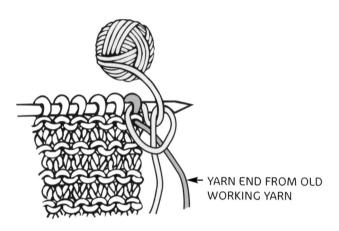

ATTACHING A NEW WORKING YARN

To start a new ball of yarn, slip the yarn end through the first stitch on the needle and knot it as shown.

← YARN END FROM OLD WORKING YARN

BINDING OFF

For an illustrated guide, see pages 16 to 18.

CASTING ON

For an illustrated guide, see pages 10 to 11.

DECREASING

Your pattern will indicate one of two ways to reduce the number of stitches in a row: by knitting or purling two stitches (two knit stitches, two purl stitches or a combination) together so they become one stitch, or by slipping a stitch to the other needle and then passing it over the stitch you just knitted or purled.

If you created an extra stitch accidentally, the best way to eliminate it is to knit (or purl) 2 together at the end of the row.

Knit 2 Together

Insert the right needle into two stitch loops and knit them together. You've just decreased the number of stitches on your needle by one.

Purl 2 Together

Insert the right needle into two stitch loops and purl them together — one purl decrease made.

Slip Stitch, Pass Slip Stitch Over

This technique will decrease with a little slant to the left, creating a pattern within a pattern.

Step 1

Knit Slip Stitch

Insert the right needle into a stitch as if you were going to knit it, but just slip it from the left needle to the right needle without knitting it.

Step 2

Pass Slip Stitch Over

Knit or purl the next stitch (depending on how the pattern reads). Use the left needle to lift the slipped stitch over the one just worked and around the tip of the right needle.

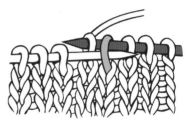

DROPPED STITCHES

For an illustrated guide to fixing, see pages 19 to 20.

EXTRA STITCHES (see DECREASING, page 60)

INCREASING

Increasing enables you to create two stitches where you only had one. There are a couple of ways to increase your stitches.

Knit Increase

Step 1

Insert the right needle into the stitch to be increased. Knit a new stitch, but don't slip the stitch off the left needle. Pull the right needle slightly to make a small loop as shown. It will now look as if you have a stitch on both needles.

Step 2

Switch the position of your needles so your right one is in back of the left one. Insert the right needle into the back of the stitch that's still on the left needle as shown and knit that stitch again, this time completing the stitch. One knit increase made!

KNIT STITCH
For an illustrated guide, see pages 12 to 13.

KNIT 2 TOGETHER (see DECREASING, page 60)

KNITTING WITH DOUBLE STRANDS
For an illustrated guide, see page 25.

PURL STITCH
For an illustrated guide, see pages 14 to 15.

PURL 2 TOGETHER (see DECREASING, page 60)

SEW THE SEAM
There are several way to join seams. Here are illustrations showing the invisible stitch, the overcast stitch, and the continuous stitch.

INVISIBLE STITCH

OVERCAST STITCH

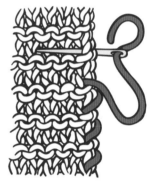

CONTINUOUS STITCH

WEAVE IN ENDS
After sewing all of the seams, hide all the loose yarn threads by weaving them into the knitted piece. If there are loose threads along a seam, thread them onto an embroidery or yarn needle and weave them through the seam or in and out of the knitted stitches along the edges of the piece on the wrong side.

If you have yarn ends that aren't near any seams, weave them through the backs of stitches (always on the wrong side) in an uneven pattern.

Index

More *Quick Starts for Kids!*® from Williamson Books!

If you like to craft, create, and keep busy with fun things to do, you may be interested in our other books. All *Quick Starts for Kids!*® books are for people of all ages — from 8 to 88! 64 pages, fully illustrated, trade paper, 8½ x 11, $8.95 U.S. softcover. To order, please see below.

More wonderful crafting ideas & how-to from Peg and Terri!

KIDS' EASY KNITTING PROJECTS

MAKE YOUR OWN COOL CARDS
25 Awesome Notes & Invitations!

REALLY COOL FELT CRAFTS

KIDS' EASY QUILTING PROJECTS

In full color!
MAKE YOUR OWN PUPPETS & PUPPET THEATERS
Also available in hardcover; $10.95 U.S.

Parents' Choice Approved
BAKE THE BEST-EVER COOKIES!

CREATE YOUR OWN CANDLES
30 Easy-to-Make Designs

KIDS' EASY BIKE CARE
Tune-Ups, Tools & Quick Fixes

40 KNOTS TO KNOW
Hitches, Loops, Bends & Bindings

Dr. Toy 100 Best Children's Products
Dr. Toy 10 Best Socially Responsible Products
MAKE YOUR OWN BIRDHOUSES & FEEDERS

GARDEN FUN!
Indoors & Out; In Pots & Small Spots

ForeWord Magazine Book of the Year Finalist
DRAWING HORSES
(that look real!)

Oppenheim Toy Portfolio Gold Award
DRAW YOUR OWN CARTOONS!

Parents' Choice Recommended
ALMOST-INSTANT SCRAPBOOKS

MAKE YOUR OWN HAIRWEAR
Beaded Barrettes, Clips, Dangles & Headbands

YO-YO!
Tips & Tricks from a Pro

BE A CLOWN
Techniques from a Real Clown

Visit Our Website!

To see what's new at Williamson and learn more about specific books, visit our secure website at:
www.williamsonbooks.com or
www.Idealsbooks.com

3 EASY WAYS TO ORDER BOOKS:

Please visit our secure website to place your order.

Toll-free phone orders: 1-800-586-2572
Toll-free fax orders: 1-888-815-2759
All major credit cards accepted (please include the card number and expiration date).

Or, send a check with your order to:
Williamson Books, Orders
535 Metroplex Drive, Suite 250
Nashville, TN 37211

Please add $4.00 for postage for one book plus $1.00 for each additional book. Satisfaction is guaranteed, or full refund without questions or quibbles.

Quick Starts for Kids!® is a registered trademark of Ideals Publications. Prices may be higher in Canada.